A Commitment to Self

The Book

Dr Kirsty Seward

Copyright © Kirsty Seward 2024

All Rights Reserved

All rights reserved. No part of this publication may be reproduced, distributed, or transmitted in any form or by any means, including photocopying, recording, or other electronic or mechanical methods, without the author's prior written permission, except in the case of brief quotations embodied in critical reviews and certain other non-commercial uses permitted by copyright law. For permission requests, please get in touch with the author.

Acknowledgements

Murphy, thank you for showing me the true meaning of unconditional love.

About the Author

Dr Kirsty Seward is a behaviour scientist from Newcastle, NSW, Australia. She has over a decade of experience in guiding women to reclaim their confidence and well-being in the health and wellness space. Her mission is to empower women to integrate a journal practice - a dedicated time for self-discovery and healing.

THIS BOOK IS A GIFT FROM MY HEART TO YOURS.

Hello beautiful,

I am so grateful this book has found its way to you – and found its home in your hands and in your heart.

In hindsight, I wasn't aware of it then, but looking back, I can now recognise that my soul has been shaping this book for you over many years. The quotes within these pages come from my own curated collection, which I've been assembling since embarking on the most transformative chapters of my healing journey in 2020. Each quote in the pages of this book has deeply resonated with me and, in some way, impacted my healing.

Beyond the transformative power of quotes, daily journaling became a ritual in my healing journey, too. And before I knew it, the quotes began steering my reflections, as I held the belief that each quote arrived at the precise moment it was meant to, shining light on areas I could further explore.

Through quotes and journaling, I'd discovered a way to connect with something beyond my physical body and mind – this is what I now know to be 'SELF'.

SELF: *your intricate and evolving fusion of thoughts, feelings, experiences, and identity that collectively shape your unique existence and perspective; it defines your sense of who YOU are and your nature of 'being'.*

I'd like to share some reflections on the title "A Commitment to SELF"...

To me, 'A commitment to SELF' has evolved into a philosophy, a foundational set of beliefs that shape the way I present myself to become the woman I am meant to be.

To me, it signifies embracing vulnerability, displaying courage, fostering curiosity, and genuinely exploring one's SELF. It involves establishing a deep connection with SELF and embracing discomfort and growth. At the core of this philosophy is the notion of compassionately embracing and nurturing all facets of your identity and individual journey, ultimately enabling your authentic SELF to radiate out into the world.

Put simply, there is no one else in this world qualified to be YOU.

To the beautiful woman who may be navigating a sense of loss and disconnection from herself, this book is for YOU.

To the woman who is in the process of unravelling, learning and redefining who she is, this book is for YOU.

To the woman who is on the quest to reconnect with her authentic self, yearning to uncover her inner strength, and cultivate unshakable self-love, this book is for YOU.

It's for you, the woman seeking to build a deep connected relationship with herself, recognising that the inward journey is what holds the key to true empowerment.

My deepest wish is that this book is the catalyst for profound change and healing. That it guides you to recognise and celebrate the woman that is uniquely and wonderfully YOU. And ultimately, it inspires you to allow her to shine.

Trust me when I say this: the world needs her magic.

All my love,

Kirst

X.

Explore this book at your own pace:

You can progress steadily through the pages day by day, or let your intuition lead, flipping to any page, trusting that the perfect quote and prompt finds you, ready to guide your reflection. Give yourself time to dive into the journal prompt. Don't overthink it; just let your pen flow.

"Our job is not to sell people on loving us. It's to be loved for simply existing as the spectacular human we were born as and to give that same kind of love back."

- Mark Groves

JOURNAL PROMPT

Think about the people in your life whom you love unconditionally. What qualities in them do you cherish without any expectations or conditions? How can you extend this same kind of love to yourself?

"The universe sends us exactly what we are ready for at the exact time we need it in our lives."

- Anonymous

JOURNAL PROMPT

Share a specific instance where you resisted a change or opportunity, only to later realise that it was exactly what you needed. How can you embrace a more open mindset moving forward?

"You are the only one in the world qualified to be you."

- Dr Kirsty Seward

JOURNAL PROMPT

Reflect on the unique qualities, skills, and experiences that make you distinctly you. What aspects of your personality or journey set you apart, and how can you celebrate and embrace them?

"Almost everything will work again if you unplug it for a few minutes. Including you."

- Anne Lamott

JOURNAL PROMPT

When was the last time you sat quietly with yourself, without the distraction of technology, such as your phone or TV?

"The beginning of freedom is the realization that you are not 'the thinker'. The moment you start *watching* the thinker, a higher level of consciousness becomes activated. You then begin to realize that there is a vast realm of intelligence beyond thought, that thought is only a tiny aspect of that intelligence. You also realise that all the things that truly matter – beauty, love, creativity, joy, inner peace – arise beyond the mind. You begin to awaken."

- Eckhart Tolle

JOURNAL PROMPT

What truly matters to me? What is important to me?

"Whoever brings you the most peace should get the most time."

- Anonymous

JOURNAL PROMPT

Reflect on the people in your life who bring you the most peace. How can you intentionally prioritise spending more time with them?

"The universe always replaces what exists in your life with something bigger and better. Don't be stuck holding onto the past or resisting change. Welcome new energy. Let go of what needs to be removed. There's great blessings in surrendering and allowing."

- Idil Ahmed

JOURNAL PROMPT

What—or who—do I need to let go of?

"Do you want to know what's extremely attractive?

Being real."

- Jake Woodard

JOURNAL PROMPT

Explore the contrast between societal ideals of 'attractiveness' and the beauty of being real. How can you redefine 'attractiveness' for yourself based on authenticity rather than external standards?

Today

"Take some time to enjoy today don't let one second of it slip away, for yesterday is gone and tomorrow's not here. Don't let a moment of today disappear."

- Peter Mann

JOURNAL PROMPT

How can I be more present today?

"When life got busier I understood that the giving of the 'gift of time' is actually real.

Spending time wisely is an art. Those who will value our time are the ones who truly understand it's importance."

- Raf

JOURNAL PROMPT

Explore the concept of 'spending time wisely is an art'. What strategies do you use to create meaningful moments in your life?

"Truth and consciousness are eternally connected.

When you tell yourself the truth, you're conscious of your thoughts, beliefs and actions.

When you're aware, you can change.

If you can change, you're free.

This is the power of consciousness, and it belongs to you."

- J.Mike Fields

JOURNAL PROMPT

Bring awareness to a belief or thought pattern that has been holding you back. How can you challenge and reframe this belief?

"Sometimes, you gotta sit and really think how blessed you are, seriously."

- Anonymous

JOURNAL PROMPT

Reflect on three things you're grateful for.

"You become what you give your attention to."

- Epictetus

JOURNAL PROMPT

How do I feel about the things I am focusing my attention on?

What do I need to focus on *less*?

What can I focus on *more*?

"Make decisions from the perspective of who you want to become."

- Anonymous

JOURNAL PROMPT

Envision yourself five years from now, fully embodying the person you aspire to be. Describe her in detail, considering attitudes, behaviours and accomplishments. How can your decisions and actions today align with this vision?

"You become a master of your life when you learn how to control where your attention goes. Value what you give your energy and time to."

- Anonymous

JOURNAL PROMPT

List three things or activities that consistently distract you or drain your energy without providing much value in return. Explore ways to redirect your focus towards more fulfilling things or activities.

"To share your weakness is to make yourself vulnerable; to make yourself vulnerable is to show your strength."

- Criss Jami

JOURNAL PROMPT

How does being vulnerable, help me build stronger and deeper relationships with others? What do I wish other people knew about me?

"It's terrifying to step outside yourself and look critically at what you do daily – finding dozens of problematic habits and the feeling of cluelessness on where to start.

Pick one you know can be handled, and don't look back at the others. You can take one and, without knowing, transform many."

- J. Mike Fields

JOURNAL PROMPT

What habit no longer aligns with the person I desire to be?
What are three actions I can take to change this habit?

"Genuine connection. That's what we're really seeking."

- Anonymous

JOURNAL PROMPT

What does 'connection' mean to me?

"Truth is, not everyone will be ready for you to 'change'. My wish for you is that you don't let the opinions of others stop you."

- Dr Kirsty Seward

JOURNAL PROMPT

Imagine your ideal version of yourself without the influence of others' opinions. What steps can you take today to align with that vision and foster self-confidence?

"It's surprising how many persons go through life without ever recognising that their feelings toward other people are largely determined by their feelings toward themselves, and if you're not comfortable within yourself, you can't be comfortable with others."

- Sidney J. Harris

JOURNAL PROMPT

Reflect on a time when your own insecurities impacted your relationships? Explore how nurturing self-compassion could enhance your relationships. What steps can you take to enhance your relationship with yourself and improve your relationships with others?

"As you evolve, notice who says,

'I'm glad I get to know this version of you'."

- Anonymous

JOURNAL PROMPT

Write about someone in your life you are grateful for.

"Funny how we see the potential in people that may not exist, yet fail to identify the power within ourselves."

- Morgan Richard Olivier

JOURNAL PROMPT

Three things that my best self would do that I'm not currently doing are...

"Every time you are tempted to react in the same old way, ask if you want to be a prisoner of the past or a pioneer of the future."

- Deepak Chopra

JOURNAL PROMPT

Write about a time where something didn't go as planned. What was your reaction? What were some new opportunities that came from the experience not going as planned?

"When you love yourself, you glow from the inside. You attract people who love, respect and appreciate your energy. Everything starts with how you feel about yourself. Start feeling worthy, valuable and deserving of receiving the best that life has to offer. Be magnetic."

- Anonymous

JOURNAL PROMPT

What are some of your insecurities? How can you start to nurture these parts of yourself?

"Raise your standards to who you want to be. And you will rise to meet them."

- J. Mike Fields

JOURNAL PROMPT

What standards do you currently hold for yourself in various aspects of your life? (Consider areas such as relationships, career, self-care and personal growth). How do these standards align with the person you aspire to be? Are there areas where you can raise your standards to better reflect your true potential?

"As soon as you truly commit to making something happen, the 'how' will reveal itself."

-Tony Robbins

JOURNAL PROMPT

What would you do right now if you knew you couldn't fail?

"Nobody wants to tell you why discipline is so important. Discipline is the strongest form of self-love. It's ignoring current pleasure for bigger rewards to come. It's loving yourself enough to give yourself everything you've ever wanted."

- Anonymous

JOURNAL PROMPT

Explore moments in your life when self-discipline felt challenging. How can you use the concept of self-love to reframe these challenges and approach them with a renewed sense of empowerment?

"Today is a great day to rediscover the art of slowness. It's all about understanding the beauty of letting things unfold organically instead of forcing things to happen."

- Anonymous

JOURNAL PROMPT

What things in my life may I be trying to force or rush? How can I slow down and embrace patience in these areas?

"Your tribe is filled with the ones who see you hit bottom and stay to hold your hand until you climb back to the top of yourself again."

- Stephanie Bennett-Henry

JOURNAL PROMPT

Write about someone in your life who has been there for you in a challenging time or through a period of growth. How did they support you, and how did this make you feel?

"Authenticity is being who you are. You aim to make your identity visible to others.

Integrity is becoming who you say you are. You strive to internalise the image you project to others.

Self-expression depends on knowing yourself. Self-expansion comes from evolving yourself."

- Adam Grant

JOURNAL PROMPT

Explore an opinion or two that you held in the past but have since questioned or changed. What led you to change that opinion?

"So, what if, instead of thinking about solving your whole life, you just think about adding additional good things. One at a time. Just let your pile of good things grow."

- Anonymous

JOURNAL PROMPT

List three things that truly bring you joy.

"You're the creator of your world.

You're the master of your experience.

And whatever you decide, so it is."

- J. Mike Fields

JOURNAL PROMPT

Explore the idea of being the creator of your own reality. What aspects of your life do you want to redesign or enhance?

Identify specific actions you can take to shape your world in alignment with your goals and values.

"For just one second, look at your life and see how perfect it is.

Stop looking for the next secret door that is going to lead you to your real life.

Stop waiting. This is it: there's nothing else.

It's here, and you'd better decide to enjoy it or you're going to be miserable wherever you go, for the rest of your life, forever."

- Lev Grossman, The Magicians

JOURNAL PROMPT

What aspects of your life are you most grateful for?

"It is 100% ok not to be who you used to be."

- Lindsey Lockett

JOURNAL PROMPT

In what ways have I grown over the past Month? Year? Decade?

"The right people will feel different to your nervous system."

- Lalah Delia

JOURNAL PROMPT

Who are the 5 people you spend the most time with? How do they make you feel?

"I owe myself an apology for when I was too busy seeking validation, I missed the most important one, my own."

- Zahra

JOURNAL PROMPT

List the things you love most about yourself.

"True self-care is not salt baths and chocolate cake, it's making the choice to build a life you don't need to escape from."

- Brianna West

JOURNAL PROMPT

What does self-care truly mean to me?

"Talk to yourself like you would to someone you love."

- Anonymous

JOURNAL PROMPT

What are three self-defeating thoughts that show up in your self-talk? How can you reframe them to be more encouraging and supportive?

"When you judge others, you do not define them, you define yourself."

- Earl Nightingale

JOURNAL PROMPT

How do you show compassion to others? How can you extend that same compassion to yourself?

"The beauty of a woman is not in the clothes she wears, the figure that she carries, or the way she combs her hair…true beauty in a woman is reflected in her soul. It's the caring that she lovingly gives, the passion that she shows, and the beauty of a woman only grows with passing years."

- Audrey Hepburn

JOURNAL PROMPT

Reflect on a woman you admire or look up to, a woman who you believe radiates 'beauty'. What are the qualities, beyond physical appearance, about her that radiate 'beauty'?

"Haters don't hate you…the reality is, they fear that they will never be able to get to where you are right now."

- Anonymous

JOURNAL PROMPT

What is a fear that I have overcome to get where I am today?

"You can literally feel when it's time to move into your life's next chapter."

- Anonymous

JOURNAL PROMPT

What are some limiting beliefs that are holding you back from stepping into your next chapter? How can you reframe these limiting beliefs to be more supportive of your journey ahead?

"You don't need to hold yourself hostage to who you used to be."

- Oprah Winfrey

JOURNAL PROMPT

What labels, negative or positive, do you assign yourself? And is it time to let these labels go?

"You, being yourself, unknowingly inspires others to be themselves."

- Mooji

JOURNAL PROMPT

Reflect on a time when someone shared that they were inspired by you.

What were you doing at the time?

How did it feel to have this positive impact on the person?

"The bravest and most inspiring people I know are the ones who are unafraid to be curious about who they are and why they show up the way they do."

- Dr Kirsty Seward

JOURNAL PROMPT

Explore a significant event in your life that helped shape who you are today.

"There comes a day when you realise turning the page is the best feeling in the world, because you realise there's so much more to the book than the page you were stuck on."

- Zayn Malik

JOURNAL PROMPT

In what ways am I holding myself back?

"You are blessed, you are amazing, you are wonderful, you are special, you are unique, you are talented, you are gifted, and you are loved."

- Asad Meah

JOURNAL PROMPT

How do you show yourself love each day?

"If you truly pour your heart into what you believe in, even if it makes you vulnerable, amazing things can and will happen."

- Emma Watson

JOURNAL PROMPT

How do I want to impact this world today?

"You're going to be the example that anything is possible and that miracles are real. Your rise will be so inspiring. Your story will show the power, the magnitude, and the magnificence of manifesting."

- Idil Ahmed

JOURNAL PROMPT

List 10 things that inspire or motivate you.

"If you don't make the time to work on creating the life you want, you're eventually going to be forced to spend a lot of time dealing with a life you don't want."

- Kevin Ngo

JOURNAL PROMPT

Think about your daily actions. Are they helping you build the life you desire? Contemplate the potential consequences of neglecting your dreams. What steps can you take today to invest in building the life you truly want?

"Who were you before the world told you who to be?"

- Dr Kirsty Seward

JOURNAL PROMPT

What advice would you give to your younger self?

"You will know your path by the way you feel."

- Anonymous

JOURNAL PROMPT

If money wasn't a factor, what would you be doing right now?

"Despite how open, peaceful, and loving you attempt to be, people can only meet you as deeply as they've met themselves."

- Matt Kahn

JOURNAL PROMPT

What three important things have you learned from previous relationships? Or friendships?

"Being true to yourself is scary and hard. Still, you must try."

- Anonymous

JOURNAL PROMPT

What is most important to you? How can you prioritise what is most important to you each day?

"Love is the strongest medicine we know."

- Anonymous

JOURNAL PROMPT

What does *love* mean to me?

"Self-confidence is earned by keeping promises to yourself."

- Robert T. Kiyosaki

JOURNAL PROMPT

Write down one thing you will do for yourself today – and then go and do it!

"That risk you're afraid to take, could be the one that changes your entire life."

- Kylie Francis

JOURNAL PROMPT

How often do you do things that get you outside of your comfort zone?

"The ego says 'once everything falls into place, I'll feel peace'.

The soul says, 'find your peace, and then everything will fall into place'."

- Marianne Williamson

JOURNAL PROMPT

Where were you, and what were you doing the last time you felt truly at peace?

"Do not be scared to say 'I love you' to yourself. Stand in front of the mirror and look at yourself and say to yourself as loudly as you can 'I love you. I respect you for what you have faced in life. And I love you for what you have become'."

- Avijeet Das

JOURNAL PROMPT

List 5 things you're proud of yourself for.

"When we are unsure of who we are, we copy.

When we are sure of ourselves, we create.

You choose."

- Leila Hormozi

JOURNAL PROMPT

Write down 3-5 goals you're currently working towards. Do your goals truly reflect your desires? Or do they reflect what someone else (a parent, partner, friend) wants for you?

"Your perception of me is a reflection of you.

My reaction to you is an awareness of me."

- Anonymous

JOURNAL PROMPT

Write about a recent situation in which you felt triggered or reactive. What was the trigger, and how did you react? What can you learn from this experience?

"When the universe gives you a new beginning, it starts with an ending. Be thankful for closed doors. They often guide us to the right one."

- Anonymous

JOURNAL PROMPT

When have you experienced a significant change in your life? What did you learn, and how can you use that knowledge to move forward?

"The beautiful thing about letting go of what is not meant for you is that you are creating space for something more exciting and new."

- Anonymous

JOURNAL PROMPT

Consider something in your life that you've recently let go of or know you need to release. How did this make you feel initially? What new possibilities do you imagine entering your life as a result of letting go? How can you embrace this sense of openness and welcome the opportunities that await you?

"Want to be happy?

Stop trying to be perfect."

- Brene Brown

JOURNAL PROMPT

When do you feel happiest in your skin?

"Life is a non-stop journey. Be proud of how far you've come, and get excited for how much further you'll go."

- Anonymous

JOURNAL PROMPT

What do you look forward to most in the future?

"Your strength doesn't come from winning.

It comes from struggles and hardship.

Everything that you go through prepares you for the next level."

- Germany Kent

JOURNAL PROMPT

What is a challenge that you have overcome? What did you learn from this challenge?

"When you let go of how life 'must be', you open the door to how it 'can be'."

- Anonymous

JOURNAL PROMPT

Reflect on a time when you 'trusted the process' rather than trying to control it. What did you learn from this?

"Being calm about everything allows your mind to find solutions. Calmness is also a state of trust. Instead of overthinking and overreacting, you just surrender for that moment and allow yourself to receive guidance for what doesn't make sense."

- Anonymous

JOURNAL PROMPT

What helps you feel calm?

"Finding more self-acceptance can open up doors for you to become a more fearless version of yourself, which can make you feel more in control of your destiny."

- Anonymous

JOURNAL PROMPT

If you fully accepted yourself for who you are, what kinds of things could you stop doing today? And what things would you start doing?

"The universe is never testing you, it's simply giving you an opportunity to practice all that you say you are."

- Maryam Hasnaa

JOURNAL PROMPT

When do you trust yourself most?

"Start doing something, you'll continue…Why? Because motivation doesn't cause action. Action causes motivation."

- Neil Pasricha

JOURNAL PROMPT

Identify one area in your life that you'd like to improve. Then, list three specific actions you can take to create that change.

"Intentional with my time.

Intentional with my energy.

Intentional with my presence.

Intentional with my love.

Intentional with me."

- Sage and Jade

JOURNAL PROMPT

What is my intention for today?

"Self-love is about slipping up, having the bad days and loving ourselves despite of them, forgiving ourselves and, most importantly, having compassion for ourselves and how we're feeling. So, give yourself permission to fall down, but don't give yourself permission to stay there."

- Saskia Lightstar

JOURNAL PROMPT

What is one thing that you can do today to show yourself kindness and compassion?

"You have to trust who you are becoming. You are not the same person you were a year ago. Allow yourself to continue to grow and evolve. Your strengths will become even stronger, your soul even more beautiful. You are magic."

- Kevin Gates

JOURNAL PROMPT

Reflect on three ways you've allowed yourself to grow this year…

"I'm thankful for my struggle because without it I wouldn't have stumbled across my strength."

- Alex Elle

JOURNAL PROMPT

Reflect on five of your strengths.

"Resist the urge to fall back into patterns that feel comfortable but are no longer good for you."

- Lacy Phillips

JOURNAL PROMPT

What part of your life have you outgrown that you are still holding onto out of fear of change? How would your life be different if you chose to release it?

"Forgive yourself for the choices you made when you didn't know you had better options. Focus on growing and moving on."

- @swaimym

JOURNAL PROMPT

What do I need to forgive myself for?

"Having high self-worth means getting comfortable being uncomfortable."

- Lacy Phillips

JOURNAL PROMPT

When you actually do get outside your comfort zone, how do you typically feel? Reflect on moments when you've stepped out of your comfort zone. What did you do? And what was the outcome?

"At some point you gotta be real with yourself about the gap between the life you want to live and the life that your daily habits are leading you towards."

- Michell C Clark

JOURNAL PROMPT

What dream or desire have you been hesitant to pursue? What's holding you back, and what steps can you take to move towards it?

"Getting what you want is knowing what you want.

Indecision is the mind-killer.

You walk in circles because there's no path forward.

Then you wake up in a year, two years, ten and your life hasn't changed at all.

If you can decide, visualise, and deeply feel something being real, time and effort are the only things stopping you.

But first…you have to decide. And say no to everything else."

- Zach Pogrob

JOURNAL PROMPT

What does your perfect day look like? Describe it in detail.

"Be you and keep being you, more you all the time. And, the bonus of showing up fully in your life is that you inspire others to do the same – you're doing all of us a favour. Authenticity is a form of service."

- Danielle Laporte

JOURNAL PROMPT

Reflect on five things that make you, you.

"The degree to which a person can grow is directly proportional to the amount of truth they can accept about themselves without running away."

- Anonymous

JOURNAL PROMPT

What is something about yourself that you absolutely know to be true?

"Ask for what you want. The worst that can happen is you receive a 'no' – the answer you were going to settle for in your silence."

- Dr Sara Kuburic

JOURNAL PROMPT

What do you feel you are not receiving enough of? Who can you ask to provide this for you? Or how can you give it to yourself?

"Visualise your best self, then show up as them. Every day. Every moment. Every choice."

- Anonymous

JOURNAL PROMPT

Describe your ideal future self.

Go into detail – get really clear.

"When we have cultivated an internal sense-of-self, we can experience rejection and know we're not flawed and need to be changed."

- Tracy Brown, RD

JOURNAL PROMPT

Think back to a time when you faced rejection or criticism and reflect on how it made you question your worth or innate value. Did it make you feel flawed or in need of change? Reflect on how cultivating a strong sense of self-worth can help you handle rejection differently. How can you strengthen your self-validation to withstand challenges without doubting yourself?

"True power is living the realisation that you are your own healer, hero, and leader."

- Yung Pueblo

JOURNAL PROMPT

What do you need in this moment? And how can you give it to yourself?

"It is absolutely necessary to flood your mind with positive thoughts about yourself."

- Iyanla Vanzant

JOURNAL PROMPT

What are your favourite parts of yourself?

"Find people who will make you better."

- Michelle Obama

JOURNAL PROMPT

Who have you spent the most time with over the past month, and how have these people influenced your life?

"Gratitude for all that's to come.

Appreciation for all that's here."

- Anonymous

JOURNAL PROMPT

Make a list of 20 things that make you smile.

"Self-awareness takes work. And listening to things you don't want to hear. And admitting that you're wrong a lot. It's not for everyone. Just for those who would rather be happier than right."

- Neil Strauss

JOURNAL PROMPT

When was the last time you realized you were wrong about something? How did it make you feel? What did you do about it?

"When was the last time you sat and gave yourself credit for how much you've grown and how far you've come? When was the last time you celebrated a relatively small win, just because? When was the last time you just sat down and said out loud, 'I'm really really proud of myself'."

- Michell C Clark

JOURNAL PROMPT

Describe a recent experience where you felt proud of yourself (no matter how 'small').

"Real transformation requires real honesty. If you want to move forward – get real with yourself."

- Bryant H. McGill

JOURNAL PROMPT

What's one thing you've been avoiding that you know you need to confront? How can you take the first step towards confronting it?

"An arrow can only be shot by pulling it backward. So when life is dragging you back with difficulties, it means that it's going to launch you into something great. So just focus, and keep aiming."

- Paulo Coelho

JOURNAL PROMPT

List five ways you can support yourself when you feel challenged…

"Trust the timing of your life. Trust your journey."

- Dr Kirsty Seward

JOURNAL PROMPT

If you fully trusted in the divine timing, how might your thoughts, feelings, attitudes and relationships change? What might you do or not do differently?

"Discipline is just self-love in motion."

- J. Mike Fields

JOURNAL PROMPT

What does your current self-care routine look like?

"Change your response to life, and your life changes."

- Anonymous

JOURNAL PROMPT

Reflect on a situation where you responded in a different way than your past self would have. How did this make you feel?

"Sit with women committed to personal growth. I promise you the conversations are different."

- Oprah Winfrey

JOURNAL PROMPT

Reflect on the conversations you have with the women in your life. Are they focused on people, ideas, or visions?

"Our entire life consists ultimately in accepting ourselves as we are."

- Jean Anouilh

JOURNAL PROMPT

What is a part of you that you struggle to accept? How can you nurture this part of you?

"Hold the vision, trust the process."

- Anonymous

JOURNAL PROMPT

Write a manifestation list to attract your dream life.

Be specific.

"Every storm runs out of rain."

- Maya Angelou

JOURNAL PROMPT

Reflect on three struggles you have overcame throughout your life. How have these helped you grow?

"When you learn to appreciate who you are right now and who you are becoming, you can leverage your personal integrity to value and keep your word."

- Lewis Howes

JOURNAL PROMPT

Consider your current age or chapter and write down three things you love about this time in your life.

Signs you are HEALING:

"More observing, less judging.

More responding, less reacting.

More self-love, less self-sabotage.

More boundaries, less resentment.

More inner peace, less outer chaos.

More clarity, less confusion.

More faith, less fear."

- Anonymous

JOURNAL PROMPT

Which *sign of healing* do you feel you've made the most progress with this year? Which *sign of healing* do you choose to intentionally focus on more going forward?

"Because true belonging only happens when we present our authentic, imperfect selves to the world, our sense of belonging can never be greater than our level of self-acceptance."

- Brene Brown

JOURNAL PROMPT

Consider one way you're unique from those around you. Why and how do you appreciate this difference in yourself?

The Importance of Gratitude

"When we choose to pause to acknowledge the beauties in our life, we are shedding a light upon the gifts we have attracted from the love we have created.

This conscious choice to look at your life with abundance brings you an awareness of how deeply worthy you are of love, belonging and joy.

Believing you are worthy of a beautiful life will make you choose authenticity and self-love above all else."

- @chantale_hl

JOURNAL PROMPT

Look around and create a gratitude list of 5 things that help you in your day-to-day life.

"Sit with it.

Instead of drinking it away, smoking it away, sleeping it away, eating it away, running from it.

Sit with it.

You gotta feel it to heal it."

- @amandaratkowski

JOURNAL PROMPT

What is something that you turn to when you need comfort? Is this serving you?

"Develop a strong opinion about yourself so that you don't accidently start believing what others say about you."

- Chetan Bhagat

JOURNAL PROMPT

When was the last time you stood up for yourself?

"What would you do to make a butterfly feel safe in your palm? Love the whole world like that. Especially you."

- Jaiya John

JOURNAL PROMPT

What's something or someone that makes you feel safe?

"Change is often a silent inside job that requires patience and courage. Courage to be yourself. Courage to resist negativity. Courage to go beyond your boundaries. Courage to take responsibility for your own life."

- Gordana Biernat

JOURNAL PROMPT

What are the steps that you have taken through the years that have made you a better version of yourself?

"You don't need to find yourself.

You're not lost.

You need to remember yourself, remember who you were before the world got to you.

That's where your power lies."

- Nikki Rowe

JOURNAL PROMPT

Take a moment to appreciate a fond memory that always brings a smile to your face.

"Courage starts with showing up and letting ourselves be seen."

- Brene Brown

JOURNAL PROMPT

What is 'courage'? What does 'courage' mean to you?

"You are important."

- Dr Kirsty Seward

JOURNAL PROMPT

Write a thank-you note to yourself.

"She's abundance in human form."

- Anonymous

JOURNAL PROMPT

When did someone smile or laugh because of you? How did this make you feel?

"Calmness is a human superpower. The ability to not overreact or take things personally keeps your mind clear and your heart at peace."

- Marc and Angel

JOURNAL PROMPT

What is your superpower?

"Yes, grow. But don't convince yourself those past versions of you were worthless. You wouldn't be here without them."

- Anonymous

JOURNAL PROMPT

Write a letter to yourself five years ago - show gratitude for this version of you.

"Joy is what happens to us when we allow ourselves to recognise how good things really are."

- Marianne Williamson

JOURNAL PROMPT

What am I grateful for in this present moment?

"Love people as they are, but also love them as they change and grow."

- John C. Maxwell

JOURNAL PROMPT

Write a paragraph about what you admire about your favourite person in the world.

"Every day, make a tiny agreement with yourself and follow through with it. You'll start to see yourself as a person who honours their word, even when no one's watching. And that's what creates true self-confidence."

- Sam Brown

JOURNAL PROMPT

How will you show up for yourself today?

"Sometimes, we form an identity around a habit that's familiar but no longer serving us.

We hold on because we don't want to lose a part of ourselves.

But that isn't who we are. It's just all we know."

- @koreen

JOURNAL PROMPT

What habits or routines no longer serve you? How can you change them to live more in alignment with who you want to be?

"First, it is an intention. Then a behaviour. Then a habit.

Then a practice. Then a second nature.

Then it is simply who you are."

- Brendon Burchard

JOURNAL PROMPT

What do I choose to embody today? (e.g. love, presence, gratitude)

"When you're grateful, you're on the frequency of receiving."

- Nika O'Neill

JOURNAL PROMPT

What *gift* have you received that mattered to you the most and why?

Steps to shift your vibration:

1. Be grateful.

2. Let go of control.

3. Start attracting instead of chasing.

4. Connect with what you love.

- Anonymous

JOURNAL PROMPT

What are three things I can do today to raise my vibration?

"Love yourself a little extra right now. You are growing, healing, learning and discovering yourself, all at once. You've got this."

- Nikita Gill

JOURNAL PROMPT

What makes me feel the most connected to myself?

"Be thankful for what you have; you'll end up having more."

- Oprah Winfrey

JOURNAL PROMPT

List 5 things in your home that you are grateful for.

"Don't overthink things. Sometimes you can convince your head not to listen to your heart. Those are the decisions you regret for the rest of your life."

- Leah Braemel

JOURNAL PROMPT

Recall a decision where you wrestled between logic and emotion, reflect on how overthinking may have led you to disregard your intuition and heart. Consider how you can find balance between honoring both your head and heart when making decisions.

"We think that accomplishing things will complete us, when it is experiencing life that will."

- Mark Nepo

JOURNAL PROMPT

When have I been able to surrender to the beauty of the moment without needing anything else?

"I will tell you again: Choose the life you want and run in that direction. Don't settle for anything else."

- F. E. Marie

JOURNAL PROMPT

When I envision my 'future best life', what's different from the life I am living right now? What steps can I take now to step into that 'future best life'?

"Life is 10% what happens to us and 90% how we react to it."

- Charles R. Swindoll

JOURNAL PROMPT

How can I support myself when I feel triggered?

"Life is short.

You get 4,000 weeks if you're lucky.

Book that flight.

Apply for that job.

Start that business.

Stop putting limits on yourself."

- Matthew McConaughey

JOURNAL PROMPT

What limitations am I putting on myself?

"Any dream is possible, if you have courage."

- Walt Disney

JOURNAL PROMPT

What is one step I can take today to bring my dreams into reality?

"If an egg is broken by an outside force, life ends. If broken by an inside force, life begins. Great things always begin from the inside."

- Jim Kwik

JOURNAL PROMPT

Which recent experience in life taught me a big lesson?

"Feeling lost?

Good!

Now you get to walk new paths that lead to much better places."

- Robin Sharma

JOURNAL PROMPT

What would I do, and where would I go if anything was possible?

"The way you speak to yourself has an enormous impact on your mood.

Try, 'I'm still learning' instead of 'I made a mistake again'.

Speak kindly to yourself, always."

- Anonymous

JOURNAL PROMPT

How do you speak to yourself when you've had a hard day? What does your inner voice sound like? Is it *critical* and *judgmental* or is it *kind* and *compassionate*? If it's critical, how can you start to change it?

"The soul should always stand ajar, ready to welcome the ecstatic experience."

- Emily Dickinson

JOURNAL PROMPT

When did something truly wonderful happen to me unexpectedly?

"When gratitude becomes an essential foundation in our lives, miracles start to appear everywhere."

- Emmanuel Dagher

JOURNAL PROMPT

Pick a random photo from your album - then write about why you're grateful for that memory.

"Giving yourself permission to have another go is where true transformation happens."

- Dr Kirsty Seward

JOURNAL PROMPT

Reflect on a time when you picked yourself up and tried again. How did this make you feel? What was the outcome?

"All I'm interested in lately is love, laughter, my personal health, growth and becoming an all-round radiant soul."

- Anonymous

JOURNAL PROMPT

When was the last time you laughed out loud? Reflect on the moment. Who was there? What made you laugh in that moment?

"You never regret the decision to invest in yourself."

- Dr Kirsty Seward

JOURNAL PROMPT

Today, I choose to invest in myself by…

"Take this opportunity to exercise the power of your imagination. Every idea begins in your mind, and if you can believe in your ability to execute, now is when you can go to the next level."

- Anonymous

JOURNAL PROMPT

What does my ideal day look like…

"Life may take you to where you least expect it, but have faith that you are exactly where you need to be."

- Julie Connor

JOURNAL PROMPT

In what ways may I be putting pressure on myself to meet society's 'timeline'. How can I honour my own timeline and my journey?

"The more you choose moves that are towards your values, the more vital, effective, and meaningful your life is likely to become."

- Susan David

JOURNAL PROMPT

My top three core values are…

Yourself first.

"Make yourself your biggest fan and best friend. Even if others aren't there to help you, you have yourself. Make sure that all of the requirements for your future are met. Make yourself a priority."

- Kevin Banag

JOURNAL PROMPT

How can I choose myself today…

"Today is full of possibilities."

- Dr Kirsty Seward

JOURNAL PROMPT

What would life feel like if I started to embrace challenges and saw them as opportunities for growth and redirection rather than seeing them as setbacks?

"You still have time

to create the you,

you want to be."

- Shane Steele

JOURNAL PROMPT

What does 'success' mean to me? What or who has influenced my definition of 'success'?

"Every person who heals themselves helps heal every person who has come before them, every person who will come after them and shows the way to everyone around them. This heals our earth. It heals our world. There is no greater work you can do."

- Sarah Alnoon

JOURNAL PROMPT

Remember a time when someone listened to you and empathized with you as you needed them to. How did this make you feel?

"The future belongs to those who believe in the beauty of their dreams."

- Eleanor Roosevelt

JOURNAL PROMPT

When I think about my dream life, what's the first thing that comes to mind?

"A girl should be two things: who and what she wants."

- Coco Chanel

JOURNAL PROMPT

In what ways have I been unauthentic and out of alignment with my true self? Why was this?

"The question isn't who's going to let me, it's who's going to stop me."

- Ayn Rand

JOURNAL PROMPT

When others doubt my potential, how can I show myself I believe in 'me'?

"You are more powerful than you know; you are beautiful just as you are."

- Melissa Etheridge

JOURNAL PROMPT

What does "beauty" mean to me?

"The strongest actions for a woman are to love herself, be herself, and shine amongst those who never believed she could."

- Anonymous

JOURNAL PROMPT

List three qualities you admire about yourself.

"Surrender to what is. Let go of what was. Have faith in what will be."

- Sonia Ricotti

JOURNAL PROMPT

Instead of worrying, I trust that no matter what happens, I…

"You miss 100% of the shots you don't take."

- Wayne Gretzky

JOURNAL PROMPT

What opportunity am I resisting, and how can I choose to embrace it instead?

"The best way to predict the future is to create it."

- Peter Drucker

JOURNAL PROMPT

What are my current life goals?

How am I working towards them?

"Mindfulness is the aware, balanced acceptance of the present experience. It isn't more complicated than that. It is opening to or receiving the present moment, pleasant or unpleasant, just as it is, without either clinging to it or rejecting it."

- Sylvia Boorstein

JOURNAL PROMPT

Reflect on a recent moment when you felt fully present and engaged. Describe the experience in detail, noting the sensations, emotions, and thoughts that arose. Consider how you can cultivate more of these mindful moments in your daily life.

"When I let go of what I am, I become what I might be."

- Lao Tzu

JOURNAL PROMPT

Am I holding onto a past version of me?

If yes, what steps can I take to let her go?

"In the middle of difficulty lies opportunity."

- Albert Einstein

JOURNAL PROMPT

Remember a time in your life that was difficult for you.

In what ways are you now thankful that the event occurred?

What did you learn or gain from the event?

In what ways might you find the positive in a

current difficult event in your life?

"You are never too old to set another goal or to dream a new dream."

- C.S. Lewis

JOURNAL PROMPT

Reflect on someone who has achieved something you desire.

What did they achieve? How did they achieve it?

What can you learn from them?

"It feels scary because it's new, not because you're incapable."

- Katie Ford

JOURNAL PROMPT

Recall a specific instance when you faced something that felt scary or intimidating, but you chose to move forward and do it anyway.

Were there any surprises or unexpected positive outcomes during or after facing the fear? What did you learn about yourself in the process?

"When you realize nothing is lacking,

the whole world belongs to you."

- Lao Tzu

JOURNAL PROMPT

I have an abundance of…

"You are not a size, you are not a number;

you are a wonderful, unique person."

- Dr. Steve Maraboli

JOURNAL PROMPT

What do you love about your body?

"Don't be pushed around by the fears in your mind.

Be led by the dreams in your heart."

- Roy T. Bennett

JOURNAL PROMPT

Consider how you can reframe fear as a source of motivation. Can fear be a catalyst for growth, pushing you to step outside your comfort zone and achieve your goals?

"Surrender isn't about being passive; it's about being open."

- Danielle LaPorte

JOURNAL PROMPT

I recognize that I don't have all the answers right now, but in my experience, I've always been guided to my highest self, including when…

"Wherever you are, be all there."

- Jim Elliot

JOURNAL PROMPT

How can I be more present in this moment?

"We're all just walking each other home."

- Ram Dass

JOURNAL PROMPT

Write a letter of gratitude to someone special in your life.

"Knowing yourself is the beginning of all wisdom."

- Aristotle

JOURNAL PROMPT

What have I learnt about myself in the past Month? Year?

"Every next level of your life will demand a different version of you."

- Anonymous

JOURNAL PROMPT

What skills is the current version of me developing, that will support the next version of me?

'Your body is not an object; it's an instrument, do not underestimate what it is capable of."

- Patricia Moreno

JOURNAL PROMPT

Show gratitude for all the ways your body carries you through each day (e.g. your heart beating for you, your arms allowing you to hug those you love)

"What if it does work out exactly how you imagined it or greater. Entertain that thought."

- T. Harv Eker

JOURNAL PROMPT

List three ways something you're working towards might actually work out far better than you ever imagined.

"The only way to live is by accepting each minute as an unrepeatable miracle."

- Tara Brach

JOURNAL PROMPT

In your final moments of life, what things will I be most grateful for?

How can I appreciate these more *today*?

"To understand and be understood, those are among life's greatest gifts, and every interaction is an opportunity to exchange them."

- Maria Popova

JOURNAL PROMPT

When was the last time you sat down and really listened to someone else with the intent to understand and not simply reply? Journal about this experience.

"In case nobody told you today.

You're worthy.

You're valid.

I'm glad you exist."

- Anonymous

JOURNAL PROMPT

Reach out to someone in your life and tell them you're grateful they exist.

"Your body is not your masterpiece – your life is."

- Glennon Doyle Melton

JOURNAL PROMPT

You are more than your body. Reflect on all the incredible qualities that you bring to the world.

"The one thing you have that nobody else has is you. Your voice, your vision. So write and draw and build and play and dance and live as only you can."

- Neil Gaiman

JOURNAL PROMPT

When was the last time you had fun? How can you add more play into your life?

"'Who does she think she is?'

A question asked by people who are genuinely perplexed at the idea of a woman living life on her own terms, enjoying her freedom, and reclaiming her power…without any apology."

- Megan Lane

JOURNAL PROMPT

Reflect on instances where you've felt judged for living life on your own terms. Explore ways to continue embracing your authenticity and confidence despite societal expectations or judgement from others.

"The next time you realise you're being too hard on yourself, think about all of the beautifully imperfect people that you love.

You accept them as they are.

You love them – flaws and all.

You deserve that kind of love. Start giving it to yourself."

- Michell C. Clark

JOURNAL PROMPT

How can I be kinder to myself?

"It's important to realise that you are living inside one of your answered prayers while you wait for your next one. There's always a place for gratitude."

- @insightfulintuitive

JOURNAL PROMPT

Look around you and find something that you can feel grateful for, no matter how small.

"In today's rush, we all think too much, seek too much, want too much, and forget about the joy of just being."

- Eckhart Tolle

JOURNAL PROMPT

When do I feel the most joy?

"You just have to have the courage to eliminate everything that doesn't directly feed what you really want."

- James Clear

JOURNAL PROMPT

What do I struggle to say no to? If I said *no* to something I normally feel obligated to do, what does that free up my time to do instead?

"The right people hear your differently."

- John C. Maxwell

JOURNAL PROMPT

Reflect on a time when you really felt heard by someone.

"Our painful experiences aren't a liability – they're a gift. They give us perspective and meaning, an opportunity to find our unique purpose and our strength."

- Dr. Edith Eger

JOURNAL PROMPT

How has your past heartbreak or losses made you stronger, wiser, more patient and more loving? Be specific and go into detail.

"Normalise silence. Work out without music, walk without your phone. Sit in a room with your thoughts, and nothing else. Magic happens when you give it space to exist."

- Zach Pogrob

JOURNAL PROMPT

When was the last time you spent time with yourself without distractions?

"Pick people who are good for your nervous system, your mind and your soul."

- Dr Sara Kuburic

JOURNAL PROMPT

Who do you surround yourself with? How do you feel after you spend time with these people?

How do you build a good life?

"Relentlessly follow your intuition. Build with people who also love to grow. Take responsibility for your healing. Love yourself so deeply that you feel at home in your own body and mind. Teach yourself to forgive. Never stop being a kind person."

- Yung Pueblo

JOURNAL PROMPT

How can you spread kindness today?

"Soul over body.

Energy over matter.

Love over fear.

Acceptance over judgement.

Higher self over ego."

- Anonymous

JOURNAL PROMPT

What does your soul crave right now?

The biggest flex:

"Putting your head on the pillow at the end of the day and being so damn proud of how you're navigating the absolute show of being human."

- Cory Muscara

JOURNAL PROMPT

Make a list of all the ways you showed yourself love today.

"You'll soon understand why your timing is perfect and

why things had to happen the way it did

to guide you to where you were meant to be."

- Idil Ahmed

JOURNAL PROMPT

For one area of your life (e.g. your career, your relationship, etc.) reflect on all the moments and experiences that have led you to where you are today. How did these moments support you to be where you are now?

"I had to make you uncomfortable, otherwise you would have never moved – *The Universe.*"

- Arjuna Ardagh

JOURNAL PROMPT

Name one time you felt uncomfortable with change. After this change, in what ways did your life get better? Or how did this change open up new opportunities for you?

"You're going to realise it one day – that happiness was never about your job, or your degree, or being in a relationship.

It was never about being like the others.

One day, you're going to see that happiness was always about the discovery, the hope, the listening to your heart and following it wherever it chose to go.

Happiness was always about being kinder to yourself.

It was always about embracing the person you were becoming. It was always about you."

- @rainbowsalt

JOURNAL PROMPT

What does happiness really mean to me?

"Self-love is the highest frequency that attracts everything that you want."

- Vironika Tugaleva

JOURNAL PROMPT

How have I chosen myself recently? How will I choose myself today?

"When 'I can do this' grows into 'I'm going to do this'…which then blooms into 'wow- I'm really doing it'."

- Sage and Jaide

JOURNAL PROMPT

What would you do today if there was no tomorrow?

"You have within you right now, everything you need to deal with whatever the world can throw at you."

- Brian Tracy

JOURNAL PROMPT

What specific situations or responsibilities are currently making me feel overwhelmed? What self-care practices can I use to navigate these feelings of overwhelm?

"Your task is not to be better than anyone else but to be better than you used to be."

- Wayne Dyer

JOURNAL PROMPT

To whom am I comparing myself to, and in what ways does their life influence the stories I construct for myself and the standards I set for my own life?

"You have been criticizing yourself for years, and it hasn't worked. Try approving of yourself and see what happens."

- Louise Hay

JOURNAL PROMPT

What would happen if I shifted my focus towards approving of myself instead of criticising? What positive changes or insights might emerge from this shift in perspective?

"Your task is not to seek for love, but merely to seek and find all the barriers within yourself that you have built against it."

- Rumi

JOURNAL PROMPT

What can I do to open my heart up to receive love more fully?

"The most loving thing we can do for the ones we love, is to take care of ourselves."

- Julia Cameron

JOURNAL PROMPT

When was the last time I took a break or gave myself some time away? How did it feel?

"Resilience is knowing that you are the only one that has the power and the responsibility to pick yourself up."

- Mary Holloway

JOURNAL PROMPT

In what areas of my life am I giving my power away to external factors? How can I take more personal responsibility for these areas?

"Do not let the behaviour of others destroy your inner peace."

- Dalai Lama

JOURNAL PROMPT

How comfortable do I feel setting boundaries with others?

"Sometimes the most important thing in a whole day is the rest we take between two deep breaths."

- Etty Hillesum

JOURNAL PROMPT

When was the last time I paused and took a deep breath?

"Beauty is the illumination of your soul."

- John O'Donohue

JOURNAL PROMPT

How has society, social media and beauty standards impacted my view of 'beauty'?

"Your body is a tool.

When you feel off, turn it on.

Walk, run, lift.

When you overthink, turn it off.

Sit, write, meditate.

Most people think their body is 'them', but it's more than that.

It's a home, and a vehicle.

For how you want to feel, and who you want to become."

- Zach Pogrob

JOURNAL PROMPT

How can I honour my body today?

"The best and most beautiful things in the world cannot be seen or even touched—they must be felt with the heart."

- Helen Keller

JOURNAL PROMPT

The "best and most beautiful things in the world" to me are…

"When it feels scary to jump, that is exactly when you jump, otherwise you end up staying in the same place your whole life."

- Abel Morales

JOURNAL PROMPT

What scares me? How can I overcome this?

"Judge each day not by the harvest you reap but by the seeds you plant."

- William A. Ward

JOURNAL PROMPT

What seeds did I plant today?

"I may not be exactly where I hope to be just yet,

But I'm grateful to be exactly where I am."

- Gary Boston

JOURNAL PROMPT

Describe your favourite moment from today.

"Always remember you matter, you're important and you are loved, and you bring to this world things no one else can."

- Charlie Mackery

JOURNAL PROMPT

What makes me feel loved and valued? How can I gift these things to myself?

"Follow your bliss."

- Joseph Campbell

JOURNAL PROMPT

If I was to listen to my authentic inner voice right now… Where would I go? What would I do? What would I say? And who would I impact?

"Communicate. Even when it's uncomfortable or uneasy. One of the best ways to heal, is simply getting everything out."

- Yung Pueblo

JOURNAL PROMPT

Reflect on a time when you had to resolve a conflict with someone or have an uncomfortable conversation. How did you approach the experience? And what did you learn that can support you to approach uncomfortable conversations in the future?

"In your journey, there will be 'in-between times' of transition. You may feel lost, confused, angry, unseen or empty.

Don't confuse these times of transition as a forever state of being or being broken. You are breaking away from what was, creating space for what will be."

- Anonymous

JOURNAL PROMPT

What are some things you want to let go of in order to make room for new opportunities?

"You're allowed to be both a masterpiece and a work in progress simultaneously."

- Sophia Bush

JOURNAL PROMPT

In what ways can I focus on progress rather than perfection?

"The only impossible journey is the one you never begin."

- Tony Robbins

JOURNAL PROMPT

What are some goals that I've been afraid to pursue due to fear of failure or rejection? What steps can I take to start pursuing these goals?

"So many doors will open for you when you decide it's okay to start over."

- Joseph Sugarman

JOURNAL PROMPT

What are some people or things that inspire you to start anew, and why?

"Every woman's success should be an inspiration to another. We're strongest when we cheer one another."

- Serena Williams

JOURNAL PROMPT

What wisdom have I learned from women in my life whom I value, and how has their wisdom enriched my life?

"There is only one way to avoid criticism: do nothing, say nothing, and be nothing."

- Aristotle

JOURNAL PROMPT

What are some ways I can seek out feedback and constructive criticism to continue growing and improving?

"Take care of your body. It's the only place you have to live."

- Jim Rohn

JOURNAL PROMPT

What is one thing I can start prioritising today that will positively impact my health…

"Every single time you set a healthy boundary in your life, you improve the relationship you have with yourself."

- Sylvester McNutt

JOURNAL PROMPT

How do I communicate my needs and boundaries in my relationships to make sure I have time and energy for self-care?

"Every exit is an entry somewhere else."

- Tom Stoppard

JOURNAL PROMPT

What new beginnings are happening in your life right now? What emotions come up for you as you start this new beginning?

"There is no old you to get back to.

There's a new you to create and nurture."

- Katie Ford

JOURNAL PROMPT

Write a letter to your future self.

"It's a terrible thing I think in life to wait until you're ready. I have this feeling now that actually no one is ever ready to do anything. There is almost no such thing as ready. There is only now. and you may as well do it now. Generally speaking, now is as good a time as any."

- Hugh Laurie

JOURNAL PROMPT

What is one creative project or new idea that I have been wanting to work on and bring to this world? What steps can I take to get started?

"Do the best you can until you know better, then when you know better, do better."

- Maya Angelou

JOURNAL PROMPT

What is one thing I've learned this past month? How can I apply this new awareness or knowledge moving forward?

"The acrobat who swings from one trapeze to the next knows just when she must let go. She gauges her release exquisitely, and for a moment she has nothing going for her but her own momentum. Our hearts follow her arc, and we love her for risking the unsupported moment."

- E. & M. Polster

JOURNAL PROMPT

When was the last time you felt completely in awe of something? Describe the moment in detail.

"I wasted so much time obsessing over what I could have been,

That I forgot about all the things that

I still

Could

Be."

- Gary Boston

JOURNAL PROMPT

If you could have any superpower today, what would it be and why?

"It is always impossible until it is done."

- Nelson Mandela

JOURNAL PROMPT

When was the last time I felt inspired? What are some things that inspire me?

"What sets you apart from the rest of the world and makes you special to me, is the suffering, tragedy, pain you have felt, yet compassion you show all and each.

This quality - rare, and lost in the world - is just what everyone needs. It's this quality in you, and you yourself, that is rare and special; unique."

- Jonathon Caukwell

JOURNAL PROMPT

Identify a challenging moment in your life and explore how it has contributed to your unique qualities of empathy and understanding.

If you're seeking support…

Explore further details about the 'Her Journal Club' community, online courses, workshops and coaching at Drkirstyseward.com.au

X.

www.ingramcontent.com/pod-product-compliance
Lightning Source LLC
Chambersburg PA
CBHW041312110526
44591CB00022B/2888